**BS EN**
# ISO 9000
# MADE SIMPLE

# BS EN
# ISO 9000
# MADE SIMPLE

John Shaw

2000

Copyright © 1995 John Shaw

First published in 1995 by
Management Books 2000 Ltd,
125a The Broadway,
Didcot,
Oxfordshire OX11 8AW
United Kingdom
Tel. +44 (0) 1235-815544
Fax. +44 (0) 1235-817188

Printed and bound in Great Britain by WBC Book Manufacturers, Bridgend

*British Library Cataloguing in Publication Data is available*

ISBN 1-85252-280-1

# CONTENTS

# PREFACE

ISO 9000 - Quality Assurance has created a plethora of fear and misunderstanding amongst a large number of company executives — much of it completely unfounded.

Horrendous tales of high costs, implementation difficulties and systems that are unworkable — particularly for smaller businesses — are common. Most are completely untrue.

ISO 9000 need not be difficult or costly to implement in any business but it is essential that the true facts are known and understood to prevent businesses adopting a negative view of Quality Assurance. Failure to understand the ethos of ISO 9000 and lack of a positive view of the significant benefits that a Quality Management System can bring to any business may well jeopardise a company's future prospects. Sitting on the fence does not make 'things happen' and in competitive market sectors failure to progress towards ISO 9000 may have a detrimental effect on a company's chances of securing new business — particularly from larger clients. Existing business may also become increasingly difficult to retain as more companies are insisting their suppliers of goods and services must have ISO 9000 accreditation.

In order to dispel fears about ISO 9000 it is vital to have a clear and simplistic understanding of all that is involved — hence the publication of this handbook, *ISO 9000 Made Simple.*

Cravenglow Consultants, one of Europe's leading ISO 9000 Quality Assurance practices, have completed large numbers of highly successful ISO 9000 projects for clients in virtually every market sector and for all types and size of business. The knowledge and expertise that has been acquired in Quality Assurance by myself and my colleagues has led me to write this handbook.

Over the years it has become apparent that ISO 9000 could be implemented more successfully if the management systems were kept simple, the documentation minimised and everyone in the business had a clear and concise understanding of Quality Assurance. ISO 9000 is no more than commercial common sense, best business practice and soundly documented controls. This handbook seeks to remove the mystique of ISO 9000 to enable you to gain a clear understanding of all that is involved.

John Shaw
*Managing Director*
*Cravenglow Consultants*

# SECTION 1

## WHAT IS QUALITY ASSURANCE?

# What is Quality Assurance?

The two words 'Quality Assurance' are probably the most frequently misunderstood in modern commercial language and it is important to dispel any misapprehensions at the outset.

Quality Assurance means providing your customer with exactly what was ordered each and every time you supply your goods or services. It is the implementation of documented controls at vital stages of your business to ensure you fulfil your customers' exact requirements. Quality Assurance must not be confused with Quality Control. Quality Control refers to the quality of the product/service you provide.

Quality Assurance is the system of documented controls within your business that ensures you never let a customer down. In other words, Quality Assurance minimises the opportunities for errors which can be costly for both you and your customer through loss of revenue — or for you, the supplier, loss of goodwill.

Loss of revenue and goodwill can occur in a number of ways:

- Late, incorrect, short deliveries which can adversely affect your customer's business
- Failure to address and correct problems quickly and efficiently
- Accepting orders you cannot complete on time and to the customer's exact specification
- Allocating tasks to inexperienced staff, which can lead to customer complaints

- Failure to inspect incoming product, which can create future problems for both you and your customer
- Lack of documented internal controls, which can affect the quality of the service you provide for your customer.

In spite of all the hype regarding the negative aspects of ISO 9000, when you take a realistic approach to Quality Assurance it soon becomes apparent that the system is good for both you and the customer. Winning and, more importantly, retaining customers has never been more difficult and the only companies that are certain of a secure future are those that do not let their customers down and continually satisfy their customer's precise requirements. Quality Assurance is good for you — and good for the customer. In the final analysis Quality Assurance is no more than commercial common sense.

ISO 9000 has been much maligned — usually by those who have little clear understanding of the ethos behind it and resent even the slightest change to working practices that may bring enormous benefits to their business. Think about the logic of ISO 9000.

Through the introduction of a policy of Quality Assurance throughout your company you will go a long way towards the elimination of errors that could cost your own company loss of revenue and possibly the loss of valuable customers. Business failures are considerably lower amongst companies that have achieved ISO 9000 accreditation.

The primary reason that you and your customers are in business is to produce a trading profit and enjoy a secure future. What can be so wrong with a Quality Assurance system that:

- Improves internal efficiency
- Minimises the possibility of costly waste and error
- Ensures total customer satisfaction
- Enhances team spirit throughout the business
- Provides a sound basis for developing new business.

My advice is this: forget those who criticise and condemn Quality Assurance — they usually do not understand *all* the positive benefits ISO 9000 can bring, and by burying their heads in the sand could be jeopardising their own company's future.

Quality Assurance does not seek to tell you how to run your company. It does not turn your business upside down by introducing controls and procedures that are both impractical and unworkable. Quality Assurance introduces sound working procedures that make commercial sense and will increase the operating efficiency of virtually every business. Through the implementation of simple yet carefully defined and documented procedures everyone in your company will be working towards the same common goal — total customer satisfaction through the elimination of errors.

# SECTION 2

## UNDERSTANDING THE INTERNATIONAL QUALITY ASSURANCE STANDARD ISO 9000

# Understanding the International Quality Assurance Standard ISO 9000

There are numerous International Standards in existence, each with its own identification number. ISO stands for International Standards Organisation and the number allocated to the one dealing with Quality Assurance is 9000. Hence ISO 9000.

ISO 9000 is subdivided into three separate Standards: ISO 9001, ISO 9002 and ISO 9003.

- **ISO 9001**

For companies involved in design, development, production, installation and servicing, ISO 9001 is of particular relevance where there is a design element, i.e. drawings or the customising of services to suit individual client requirements, as with oil pipeline design, architects or accountants.

- **ISO 9002**

This is the most widely implemented section of the International Standard and is applicable to all companies involved in production, installation and servicing but where there is no specific design element involved. It is relevant to all companies manufacturing goods and/or offering a service. Stockists and distributors also fall into this category.

## • ISO 9003

The least used section of the Standard, this is applicable only to companies where conformance to specified requirements is to be confirmed by the supplier at final inspection and test.

For the vast majority of businesses ISO 9002 will be the section of the Standard that will usually be applicable.

The International Standard is a 10-page document that requires 20 sections to be addressed by any business implementing a Quality Assurance policy.

ISO 9000 was initially published in 1979, and from a slow start it is now being implemented by a very large number of commercial organisations. In fact, increasingly many companies are now insisting that their suppliers of goods and services must implement ISO 9000 if trading relationships are to be maintained.

ISO 9000 is applicable to any type of business, regardless of number of staff, turnover or market sector. It is becoming increasingly important for exporters — particularly those selling into European markets.

Successful ISO 9000 accreditation is a positive and highly valuable accolade that advises other commercial enterprises that you are a well organised, efficient organisation that manages the vital stages of the business through documented procedures and that total customer satisfaction is the primary consideration.

# SECTION 3

## THE INTERNATIONAL STANDARD
## ISO 9000 EXPLAINED

# The International Standard ISO 9000 Explained

Each of the 20 sections of ISO 9000 that must be addressed is prefixed by the number 4 and they run consecutively from 4.1 to 4.20 with a number of subsections. These will be described in detail below and form the basis of the two manuals that must be prepared — Quality Policy and Operational Procedures. These are the documentary proof of an organisation's dedication to the implementation of Quality Assurance and the implementation methods they use.

## The Quality Policy Manual

This Manual is a statement of the company's commitment to a Quality Assurance Policy and must include all relevant sections and subsections of the International Standard where they apply to an individual business.

While the 20 vital sections of the Standard begin at number 4 there are three introductory sections that must be written into the Quality Policy Manual.

### 1 Scope

The Manual should define the nature of the company's goods or services that are seeking accreditation.

(Companies may themselves decide which of their specific goods, services or operations are to be assessed if a total company accreditation is not being sought.)

## 2 Normative Reference

Any Standards, including ISO 9000, used by the company as reference points must be listed in this section. The organisation must also have an up-to-date copy of any Standards on file.

## 3 Definitions

The following text should be included in all Quality Policy Manuals:

### 3.1 Product

A product may include service, hardware, processed materials and software, or any combination thereof.

A product can be tangible (e.g. assemblies or processed materials) or intangible (knowledge or concepts), or a combination thereof.

The term product refers to the intended product offering and not to any unintended 'by-product' which may affect the environment.

### 3.2 Tender

The offer made by the company in response to an invitation to satisfy a contract award to provide a product.

### 3.3 Contract

An agreement between the company and a customer to supply the customer's agreed requirements which can be transmitted by any means.

## The Operational Procedures Manual

While the Quality Policy Manual is a statement of the company's intention to pursue Quality Assurance, the

Procedures Manual and accompanying documentation
confirm how ISO 9000 is actually implemented throughout the business.

# SECTION 4

## QUALITY SYSTEM REQUIREMENTS

# 4.1 Management Responsibility

## 4.1.1 Quality Policy

Under this section the company must define its commitment to a Quality Policy with a quality statement — for example:

> In our company the experience, attitude and skill of our staff are our main assets. These three key elements are essential to the continuing success of our business.
>
> It is our aim to improve constantly the quality of the service we provide to enhance customer satisfaction.

This Quality Policy statement should be printed, framed and hung in the company's reception area where it is visible to staff and customers. It should be signed by the Managing Director and/or Quality Manager.

The Quality Policy must be understood and implemented by every member of staff regardless of their position within the organisation.

## 4.1.2 Organisation

### 4.1.2.1 Responsibility and Authority

Sound organisation of the business is vital if a successful policy of Quality Assurance is to be implemented. An organisational chart should be created, using job titles and not individual names, to detail how the business is structured and outlining areas of responsibility.

Of particular importance is the designation of departmental heads who will have specific responsibility for ensuring the smooth operation of the Quality System within the section of the company under their control. Departmental heads are responsible for initiating action to prevent non-conformances. A non-conformance occurs when something goes wrong — in other words, when a problem or error arises.

Non-conformances can occur in one or a combination of the following:

- Product or service fault
- Problem created by a supplier
- Breakdown or error in the Quality System.

The departmental head must:

- Identify and record any quality problems (non-conformance reports).
- Initiate action or suggest improvements to prevent future non-conformances. This may involve liaison with the senior management or other departmental heads.
- Check solutions are effective. If the initial corrective action taken is subsequently found to be inadequate then alternative corrective action must be taken.
- Control further processing, delivery or installation of any non-conforming product until the deficiency has been corrected.

In other words, each departmental head has the responsibility for identifying and correcting non-conformances and then checking that the corrective action taken is actually working.

### 4.1.2.2 Resources

The company must implement a system for checking and proving that the Quality System is working efficiently by regular internal audits. An audit is a documented check of all procedures and documentation used by the company to identify current problems or trends that may lead to future non-conformances.

Only suitably trained or qualified personnel should be allocated to undertake work that could affect the ultimate quality of the company's product or service. At least one internal auditor must be appointed who will check the systems and documentation are working effectively. These checks should be undertaken at least twice a year to identify any problems. Staff undertaking audits and those with managerial/supervisory responsibilities must receive ongoing training in ISO 9000 procedures. Details of ISO 9000 training must be entered on individual Training Records.

### 4.1.2.3 Management Representative

Every business implementing ISO 9000 must appoint a Quality Assurance Manager (Management Representative) who, irrespective of other duties, will be responsible and have the authority for coordinating and monitoring the Quality System to ensure all aspects of ISO 9000 are fully implemented and maintained in accordance with the International Standard.

The Quality Manager must liaise constantly with the company's senior management on the performance of the Quality System.

### 4.1.3 Management Review

Management Review means a properly convened meeting to discuss all matters relating to Quality Assurance and the effectiveness of the system. Those present should be the directors and the Quality Assurance Manager, although departmental heads and anyone else whose work affects quality issues may be invited to attend.

An agenda should be produced in advance of the meeting and minutes recorded as part of the Quality System documentation. At least one Management Review must be held each year but more frequent meetings — monthly — are recommended.

## Summary of Section 4.1

1. Prepare a Quality Policy.

2. Detail a company organisation chart.

3. Record departmental responsibilities and authorities.

4. Ensure staff are trained in all aspects of Quality Assurance — particularly auditing techniques.

5. Appoint a Management Representative (Quality Assurance) Manager.

6. Hold regular Management Reviews (Quality Assurance Meetings).

# 4.2 QUALITY SYSTEM

## 4.2.1 General

A fully documented Quality System must be implemented and documented, which will involve a limited amount of new paperwork for most companies. Documentation is essential to:

- Control the Quality System effectively
- Ensure that the product or service conforms to specified requirements
- Prove to the accreditation body that you have implemented and control the Quality Assurance System in accordance with the requirements of ISO 9000.

Documenting the Quality System ensures all staff understand the ethos of ISO 9000. A Quality Manual must be produced covering all elements of the International Standard, including the procedures for implementing the Standard and the documents used in the system.

## 4.2.2 Quality System Procedures

The following procedures must be addressed, documented and controlled through the implementation of a Quality Assurance System:

1. Designation of areas of responsibility and authority within the organisation — particularly relating to matters affecting quality

2. Procedures to ensure customers' requirements can be fully satisfied, i.e. correct specification, on-time deliveries, etc.

3. Control of any amendments to the customer's requirements to eliminate the chances of incorrect delivery or installation of the product or service

4. Ensure all documentation used throughout the company is up to date and fit for use by the relevant personnel

5. Control of suppliers to ensure goods/services purchased are correct and fit for purpose

6. All suppliers are assessed for suitability to satisfy exact requirements and/or specifications

7. A system of traceability to source — identifying which supplier provided individual products should there be a product fault or problem. Organisations must also be able to trace items to production batches, individual operatives or machines according to the nature of their product or service.

8. Tasks are allocated to personnel with adequate skills and training to complete work satisfactorily and all work instructions are clear and unambiguous

9. Procedures to inspect and test product:
   - from suppliers (Receiving, Inspection and Testing)
   - during production/installation (In-Process Inspection and Testing)
   - following production/installation (Final Inspection and Testing)

10. Any equipment used for measuring, inspecting or

testing must be calibrated at predetermined intervals and inspection criteria recorded

11. All orders must be handled with care, stored, checked and delivered in sound condition to the customer

12. Any non-conforming product must be isolated to prevent it inadvertently entering the supply chain

13. Adequate stocks must be held to ensure customers' requirements can be satisfied

14. Corrective action must be taken to rectify and prevent further problems of a similar nature arising

15. A Quality Assurance Manager must be appointed (Management Representative)

16. Ongoing staff training is essential — using internal and if necessary external agencies. All staff must receive training in Quality Assurance issues and the key role they play in ensuring the effectiveness of the system

17. All Quality Records must be maintained and stored for a minimum of three years.

These elements are the essential and vital components for every Quality System, regardless of the type or size of business. Failure to address and document them all may lead to an unsuccessful accreditation.

Initially there seems a great deal to consider but when each requirement of the International Standard is implemented it is surprising how quickly the Quality System will begin to operate efficiently. Maintaining the system will become a normal operating procedure and any initial fears and misconceptions will soon be dispelled.

ISO 9000 brings many benefits to those organisations who have successfully implemented a Quality Assurance System, including tighter internal controls which lead to greater efficiency and the reduction of potentially costly errors. ISO 9000 is also a wonderful marketing tool — particularly when developing new business.

## 4.2.3 Quality Planning

It is important to define and document how the requirements for quality will be achieved through Quality Planning that is consistent with the Quality System and compatible with normal operating procedures.

Quality Planning is particularly relevant where customers' specific requirements must be fulfilled, such as specified product requirements and projects or contracts. In these circumstances it is necessary to prepare a Quality Plan which details how customers' specific requirements will be achieved. This may include the identification or acquisition of:

- Controls
- Processing methods
- Equipment (including inspection and test equipment)
- Fixtures
- Resources and skills

that are necessary to achieve the required quality. Quality Planning also involves (where relevant to the project):

- Ensuring the design, production process, installation, servicing and inspection and test procedures are compatible and controlled by the relevant documentation
- It may be necessary to update quality control and inspection and testing procedures to ensure project compliance and in certain circumstances the development of new instrumentation may be required
- The identification of any measurement requirement involving capability that may exceed the known state of the art in sufficient time for the required capability to be developed

- Verification stages must be identified at appropriate stages in the realisation of the product
- Standards of acceptability must be clarified for all features and requirements, including those which contain a subjective element
- All Quality Records which form part of the Quality Plan must be completed and retained as part of the company's overall Quality Records (see Section 4.16)

## Summary of Section 4.2

1. All 20 elements of the International Standard must be addressed.

2. Each aspect of the Quality System must be fully documented.

3. In relevant circumstances a documented Quality Plan must be produced.

# 4.3 CONTRACT REVIEW

## 4.3.1 General

In all instances every contract or order must be documented and checked to ensure the supplier has the capability of fulfilling all aspects of the customer's requirements.

## 4.3.2 Review

Before submitting a tender or accepting an order the supplier must ensure that:

- The customer's exact requirements are defined and understood and documented and that there are no ambiguities. The same criterion applies where verbal orders are received.
- Any differences between the contract or order requirements and those in the tender are resolved
- The supplier must ensure the capability exists to fulfil the contract or order requirements.

It is recommended that all enquiries and invitations to tender are fully recorded to eliminate possibilities of error. It is also recommended that all quotations are confirmed in writing to avoid misunderstandings between the customer and the supplier. A policy of constant liaison with the customer is advisable to prevent problems of a serious or potentially costly nature arising.

## 4.3.3 Amendment To a Contract

Should a customer amend his order or contract requirements the supplier must adequately document such changes and ensure that all relevant individuals and/or departments are aware of the amendments. This can be achieved by altering all copies of the original order/contract or raising a new order or contract detailing the revised customer requirements, but ensuring the original order is removed from the system.

## 4.3.4 Records

All contract review details form part of the organisation's Quality Records (see Section 4.16) and must be maintained for a minimum three-year period.

## Summary of Section 4.3

1. Record all enquiries on an Enquiry Form or Register which may also be used for individual order costing purposes.

2. Ensure the capability exists to satisfy the customer's exact requirements and that these are fully documented and there are no issues that could lead to a misunderstanding or error.

3. Any differences between the order and the original quotation or tender must be discussed and resolved.

4. Confirm all quotations in writing.

5. Document any changes to the customer's requirements by (a) amending the original order or (b) raising a new order, ensuring all relevant departments are aware of the amended requirements.

6.  Maintain constant customer liaison.

7.  Retain Contract Review documentation as an integral part of the Quality Records.

# 4.4 DESIGN CONTROL

This section of the International Standard should be addressed only by organisations seeking ISO 9000 - Part 1 accreditation. For companies seeking ISO 9000 - Part 2 or Part 3 accreditation the heading '4.4 Design Control' should be written into both the Quality Policy and Operational Procedures Manuals with the comment 'Not Applicable'. This procedure will ensure that the Manuals follow the exact section numbering requirements of the International Standard.

## 4.4.1 General

Documented procedures must be established to control and verify the design of a product or service to ensure customers' exact requirements can be met.

## 4.4.2 Design and Development Planning

A detailed plan should be prepared for each design or development activity and must identify who is responsible for their implementation.

Design and development activities should be allocated to suitably trained and qualified personnel who have the expertise and resources to fulfil the customer's requirements and who will be responsible for updating plans, drawings or project terms of reference as the circumstances require.

### 4.4.3 Organisational and Technical Interfaces

Where different groups or separate technical departments in an organisation are required to have an input into project design and development, such groups and/or departments are identified with the information they require documented, transmitted and regularly reviewed.

### 4.4.4 Design Input

Design input requirements for the product or service must be identified, documented and their adequacy checked, for example, with a view to statutory or regulatory requirements.

Where there are initial design input differences or misunderstandings or incomplete information these will be resolved with those responsible for imposing these requirements. Design input must also take into account contract or order requirements and any subsequent amendments.

### 4.4.5 Design Output

Completed drawings of product or service designs must be documented in such a manner that they can be checked and validated against the customer's original requirements. A Design Output Control Sheet is recommended to record the following:

- Original design requirements have been satisfied
- Drawings or documents contain or make reference to acceptance criteria
- Identify the vital characteristics of the design that are crucial to the safe and correct functioning of the product — for example, operating methods, storage requirements.

All completed design documents and drawings must be checked before release.

## 4.4.6 Design Review

At predetermined stages of the design formal and documented checks must be undertaken to ensure ongoing conformity to the customer's requirements. Relevant members of staff from all departments involved in the design process must be involved in the review process and, where required, any other specialist personnel. Design reviews must be documented and form part of the organisation's Quality Records (see Section 4.16).

## 4.4.7 Design Verification

At each vital stage in the design process checks must be undertaken to ensure that the initial design requirements are being satisfactorily completed. Such checks must be recorded and form part of the Quality Records (see Section 4.16).

Additionally, Design Reviews may include:

- Performing alternative calculations
- Comparing the new design with a similar proven design
- Undertaking tests or demonstrations
- Checking design stage documents before release.

## 4.4.8 Design Validation

Design validation checks must be undertaken to ensure the product or service conforms to the customer's needs or requirements.

## 4.4.9 Design Changes

All design changes or modifications must be identified, recorded, checked and approved by authorised personnel before they are implemented.

## Summary of Section 4.4

1.  All procedures relating to a product or service design must be established to ensure the customer's exact requirements can be met.

2.  Prepare a detailed plan for each design or development activity, identifying who is responsible for implementation.

3.  Only suitably qualified or experienced personnel should be allocated design activities.

4   Organisational and technical interfaces must be identified and information flow controlled and documented.

5.  Ensure design controls reflect statutory or regulatory requirements.

6.  Any design amendments must be reviewed and documented.

7.  Completed drawings or designs must be checked against the customer's initial requirements. A Design Control Sheet is recommended.

8.  Identify the vital design characteristics that are essential for sound operating performance or storage requirements.

9.  All completed drawings and designs must be checked before release and the individual responsible for their release identified.

10. Checks must be completed at all vital stages of the design process to ensure conformity to customer's requirements. Relevant members of staff from all appropriate departments should be involved in the Design Review.

11. Designs and drawings must be regularly checked at

each stage to ensure the initial design requirements are being satisfied. These checks must be documented and recorded on the Design Control Sheet.

# 4.5 DOCUMENT AND DATA CONTROL

## 4.5.1 General

This section of the Standard refers to the control of all internal documentation that relates to the International Standard — i.e. purchase order forms, delivery notes, job cards. It also refers to any other vital documents that are essential for ensuring the essential controls of the business — for example, work instructions, data sheets, the Quality Assurance Manual and Operational Procedures Manual and the Quality Management documentation.

Documented controls must also be exercised over all relevant external documentation, such as Standards, drawings and statutory regulations.

## 4.5.2 Document and Data Approval and Issue

The Quality Assurance Manager is responsible for ensuring that all vital documents are recorded in a Document Control Register and that they are fit for purpose. All documents must be identified on the Document Control Register by their user. Should a departmental head wish to alter a document then such changes must be agreed with the Quality Manager.

## 4.5.3 Document and Data Changes

When a document becomes obsolete through updating or an amendment to operating procedures it must be removed from circulation and replaced with the new document.

With ISO 9000 it is no longer sufficient just to alter documents — changes must be recorded to ensure all relevant personnel are using the current form.

Documents are the vital controls in every organisation. They are also essential for proving to an accreditation body that you are operating a satisfactory Quality Assurance system.

### Amendments to the Quality and Operational Procedures Manuals

All changes to the Quality and/or Operational Procedures Manuals are the responsibility of the Quality Manager in consultation with departmental heads. All amendments must be recorded by the Quality Manager and obsolete pages removed and replaced by the updated versions.

## Summary of Section 4.5

1. All internal and relevant external documents must be recorded in a Document Control Register.

2. Other vital documents must also be recorded, including the name of the holders.

3. All document changes must be agreed with the Quality Manager and recorded.

4. Obsolete documents must be removed from the system.

5. Changes in the Quality Policy and Operational Procedures Manuals must be recorded and the obsolete pages removed and replaced.

6. Any obsolete documents retained for legal and/or knowledge preservation purposes must be identified.

# 4.6 PURCHASING

## 4.6.1 General

Purchasing is a vital function for most companies and as such must be rigorously controlled. Major problems arise when purchased goods or services fail to satisfy exact requirements. A chain reaction effect may seriously influence the ability to satisfy customers' exact requirements.

It is essential to ensure that all purchased goods and services conform in every way to stated requirements. Errors can be costly in terms of lost time, inadequate finished product and erosion of credibility with the customer. Documented procedures must be implemented to ensure purchased product or service conforms to specified requirements.

## 4.6.2 Evaluation of Subcontractors

It is mandatory for an assessment to be made of all suppliers of goods and services that could directly affect the provider's product or service. They must be evaluated on their ability to satisfy specific requirements, including Quality Assurance.

A simple questionnaire must be sent to all suppliers to ascertain:

- If they are ISO 9000 accredited
- If they operate their own Quality Assurance system
- Their location
- The nature of the goods and services they supply
- The name of the Quality Manager.

When questionnaires are returned the detail should be entered in a Suppliers' Register.

All suppliers should be graded 1-3 according to the information provided in the questionnaire:

- Grade 1 —the supplier has ISO 9000 or equivalent

- Grade 2 —the supplier does not have ISO 9000 but has a satisfactory performance level achieved over a minimum six-month period

- Grade 3 —a new or probationary supplier without ISO 9000. Such companies may be upgraded to Grade 2 after six months if an acceptable performance level has been achieved.

The Subcontractors' Register forms part of the organisation's Quality Records (Section 4.16).

## 4.6.3 Purchasing Data

All purchasing documents must state clearly exact requirements. There must be no room for ambiguity — this is when mistakes can occur. It is therefore essential to complete a Purchase Order Form detailing exact requirements, which should be faxed or mailed to suppliers each time an order is placed.

Purchase Order Forms should also be used for checking against suppliers' Delivery Notes to ensure exact requirements have been fulfilled.

## 4.6.4 Verification of Purchased Product

### 4.6.4.1 Supplier Verification at Subcontractor's Premises

When the supplier checks purchased product at the Sub-contractor's premises the supplier must specify how such checks will be undertaken and how product will be released and identified in the purchasing documents.

### 4.6.4.2 Customer Verification of Subcontracted Product

When it is specified in a contract, the customer should be allowed to visit the supplier's premises to check the product conforms to requirements. These checks do not absolve the supplier of the responsibility to maintain effective control of the product and ensure it continues to meet the customer's requirements. It does not preclude subsequent rejection by the customer.

## Summary of Section 4.6

1.  Assess your suppliers by using a questionnaire.

2.  Record all vital purchasing information on a Purchase Order Form.

3.  Send the Purchase Order Form to suppliers.

4.  Record the supplier's information in a Subcontractors' Register.

5.  Grade suppliers 1-3.

6.  Visit suppliers' premises to verify the product fulfils exact requirements if this is deemed necessary.

7.  Customers should be allowed to inspect product at the supplier's premises but this does not absolve the supplier of responsibility for undertaking all relevant checks before despatch to the customer.

# 4.7 CONTROL OF CUSTOMER-SUPPLIED PRODUCT

On occasion goods may be supplied by the customer — for example, for incorporation into supplies or related activities or to provide the metal for fabricating — or it may be that the supplier provides components, drawings, etc. In all such instances items must be separately recorded and controlled to prevent loss or damage and must be stored separately, identified and segregated from the supplier's own stock. The customer must be notified if product is lost or damaged and the details recorded as part of the Quality Records (Section 4.16).

An initial check to ensure the goods supplied are fit for use should be undertaken but this does not absolve the customer from the responsibility to provide acceptable product.

## Summary of Section 4.7

1. Where goods are supplied by the customer a documented system to control them must be implemented.

2. Such items must be recorded.

3. Controls should be implemented to prevent loss, damage or deterioration.

4.  They should be identified and stored separately so they are not inadvertently mistaken for the company's own stock.

# 4.8 PRODUCT IDENTIFICATION AND TRACEABILITY

This section of the International Standard is applicable to two sectors of most organisations.

1.  Components or other purchased goods or services must be traceable to the company supplying the product. This is particularly important where items from different suppliers may have similar characteristics of design and performance. They must be clearly identified and stored separately.

2.  All finished product must be traceable to the customer's original requirements. This can be achieved through markings, documentation or other means that ensure product without fault is correctly supplied to the customer. Traceability can also be achieved through lot or batch numbers. Details must be recorded and form an integral part of the organisation's Quality Records.

Traceability is vital to minimise and correct problems. For example, a supplier has had a manufacturing fault that has not been detected by his own inspection procedures and this product has created problems. The ability to identify the supplier of such product means that unsuitable items can be segregated, removed by the supplier for rechecking and, if necessary, replaced.

The implementation of a system of product identification and traceability is essential at all stages of:

* Receipt
* Production
* Delivery of product or service
* Installation.

Product identification and traceability will enable faults to be corrected quickly and effectively and minimise potential problems with customers.

At every stage of the process procedures must be implemented to ensure total traceability of items produced and for components or services supplied by sub-contractors. Traceability methods vary and procedures that best suit individual operations should be implemented.

Batch identification ensures that if a faulty item is identified the entire batch can be rechecked to prevent other non-conforming products reaching the supply chain.

## Summary of Section 4.8

1. Purchased products or services must be traceable to their immediate supplier.

2. Manufactured product must be traceable to raw material suppliers, production batches and, where appropriate, to a specific machine or operative.

3. Traceability minimises the opportunity for further problems with product and/or services.

4. Traceability is vital at all stages of the organisation and must be controlled by documented procedures.

# 4.9 Process Control

All stages of production, installation or servicing must be documented and controlled to prevent error. Such controls ensure the customer's exact requirements are fulfilled.

Work instructions must be issued to eliminate confusion and all jobs should only be allocated to staff with the skill and experience required to complete the work satisfactorily.

All production should be planned in advance to ensure compliance with customers' product and delivery criteria.

Processing equipment should be fit for the purpose and properly maintained to ensure minimum down-time and to ensure manufactured items will satisfy customers' requirements.

Vital production stages should be identified together with hold points. These should be documented to ensure that any product faults can be identified at the earliest opportunity and corrective action taken. This process control is essential to eliminate problems which could lead to:

- Loss of production time
- Wasted material
- Rework time

which could seriously inconvenience the customer. Any special processes should also be fully documented to minimise production problems.

If processing checks cannot be checked before product is despatched to the customer and deficiencies may be later identified, only suitably skilled operators can be used and constant monitoring implemented.

Lack of effective process controls can be costly. Documented procedures will prevent such losses.

## Summary of Section 4.9

1. All stages of the production/installation or provision of the service process must be controlled through adequate documentation.

2. Work instructions should be issued and where necessary it is essential to comply with quality plans and reference standards.

3. Pre-plan production.

4. Allocate work only to suitably skilled staff.

5. Ensure processing equipment is fit for the purpose.

6. Correct maintenance of all processing and associated equipment is essential.

7. Identify and control all the vital stages of production together with product characteristics and processing parameters.

8. Any special processes should be documented and implemented only by suitably qualified staff and equipment.

# 4.10 INSPECTION AND TESTING

## 4.10.1 General

This section of the Standard refers to three distinct inspection and testing operations. Each one must be fully documented to ensure the product, installation or service quality characteristics are being met and that customers' exact requirements are being fulfilled.

## 4.10.2 Receiving Inspection and Testing

**4.10.2.1**  All product supplied must be checked before it is used or processed to ensure:

- Purchase Order requirements in terms of quality, quantity and product specification have been satisfied
- Where necessary tests or visual inspection to confirm product compliance with specification will be undertaken to ensure purchased goods are in sound condition
- Product must not be allowed to enter the production cycle or be taken into stock without documentary evidence of checking on receipt

**4.10.2.2**  The amount of checking on receipt of purchased product may depend on previous checks undertaken at the supplier's premises. Such checks must be fully documented.

**4.10.2.3**   Where purchased product is urgently required and has not been fully checked such items must be clearly recorded to allow immediate recall if they prove to be faulty.

## 4.10.3 In-Process Inspection and Testing

Checks must be implemented at each stage of the production or installation process or delivery of the service to ensure product conforms to requirements.

All product must be held until the required inspection tests have been completed. Checks must be documented. Where checks are not undertaken product should be released under a positive-recall procedure and clearly identified.

Product can only pass to the next stage of production, installation or delivery of the service if there are no problems recorded.

## 4.10.4 Final Inspection and Testing

Final checks must be undertaken and recorded prior to the release of product to the customer. This is the final proof that there are no identifiable problems and product satisfies the customer's requirements. Should final inspection and test procedures highlight a problem non-conforming items must be isolated to prevent them from inadvertently entering the supply chain and reaching the customer.

## 4.10.5 Inspection and Test Records

The three inspection and test stages detailed must all be fully recorded as evidence that product:

• Satisfies predetermined specification (conforming) or
• Fails at any of the three inspection and test procedures (non-conforming).

## Summary of Section 4.10

1. All incoming product must be checked to ensure its suitability.

2. Unsuitable product must not be allowed to enter the production process or be taken into stock.

3. During production checks must be made at all the vital manufacturing stages to ensure product is conforming to specified requirements.

4. Following production and prior to release of goods to the customer final inspection and test checks should be implemented and documented.

5. Non-conforming product identified at any stage of the process should be isolated until a decision is made regarding disposition.

6. A quarantine area in the warehouse should be allocated to hold non-conforming product until a decision regarding its disposal is made.

7. All checks must be recorded and retained for a minimum three-year period as part of the company's Quality Records.

# 4.11 CONTROL OF INSPECTION, MEASURING AND TEST EQUIPMENT

## 4.11.1 General

It is of paramount importance to make a detailed analysis of all equipment used in the manufacturing or installation processes. Any item of equipment, including test hardware and software, used for:

- inspection
- measuring
- testing

must be identified and recorded in a Calibration or Plant and Equipment Register.

## 4.11.2 Control Procedure

All such items of equipment used for any or all of these procedures must be:

- calibrated
- controlled
- checked

at specific, predetermined intervals. This is applicable to all equipment owned by the company or provided by an outside source.

All equipment and the calibration tests undertaken must be recorded and detailed information provided regarding the standards, testing criteria and tolerance against which the equipment is being checked. The individual authorising the nature and scheduling of the checks must be identified.

Test hardware and software, when used in the inspection process, must be checked to ensure it is capable of verifying the acceptability of the product prior to release for production, installation or servicing.

Any item of inspection, measuring or test equipment that fails a calibration check must be the subject of a non-conformance report and must not be used again until it satisfies the tolerances against which it is being checked. Environmental conditions must be suitable for calibration tests and all such equipment must be handled and stored appropriately to ensure testing accuracy is maintained.

## Summary of Section 4.11

1. Record all items of equipment that are used for inspection, measuring or testing in a Calibration Register.

2. Detail the frequency of the checks, nature of the checks and against which standards or tolerances the checks are being made. All details must be entered in a Calibration Register, which can double up as a Plant and Equipment Register.

3. All designated equipment, whether or not it is owned by the company, must be subjected to calibration checks.

4. Outside specialists may be used for performing some of the calibration checks.

5. Should a piece of equipment fail to meet the required calibration standard, it must not be used again until the problem has been corrected and a

satisfactory re-test has been completed and documented.

6.  Test hardware and software must also be checked.

7.  Environmental conditions must be suitable for calibration checks.

8.  Inspection, measuring and testing equipment must be handled and stored appropriately to maintain testing accuracy.

# 4.12 INSPECTION AND TEST STATUS

The status of the product or service must be clearly identified at all stages of the production or installation process. Product is identified in one of two ways:

1. Conforming to specification
   or
2. Fails to meet the required specification (non-conforming).

Formalised control procedures are essential to prevent non-conforming product moving to:

- The next stage of the process
  or
- Being released to the customer.

Such controls ensure that only product meeting the required specification is released to the customer. The procedures detailed in Section 4.10 (Inspection and Testing) will identify when there is a product non-conformance.

At all times documentary proof is required that the product has been:

- Approved through the inspection processes
- Not inspected
- Inspected and failed.

The individual responsible for ensuring that all inspection and test procedures have been undertaken must be identified together with a record of who authorises conforming product to move to the next stage of the process, installation or for despatch to the customer.

Items failing to meet the required specification at any of the processing control points should be clearly identified by:

- Markings
- Authorised stamps
- Tags/labels
- Being moved to a quarantine area clearly labelled 'Do Not Use'.

It must be fully understood why such checks are undertaken. If non-conforming product is released to the next stage of production or to the customer serious quality problems can arise which may create costly complications for both supplier and customer. Documented checks identify problems before they become uncontainable.

## Summary of Section 4.12

1. The status of the product or service — conforming or non-conforming — must be identified at all stages of production/installation or delivery of the service.

2. Formal written procedures must be implemented to prevent non-conforming product from being further processed or released to the customer.

3. Only conforming product can be released to the next stage of the process or to the customer.

4. The person with the authority to authorise release of conforming product to the next stage of production or to the customer must be named.

5. Items failing to meet the required specification must

be identified, marked and removed from the system and, where applicable, stored in a quarantine area to await disposal.

# 4.13 CONTROL OF NON-CONFORMING PRODUCT

## 4.13.1 General

Section 4.12 determined the status of the product as conforming or non-conforming. The control of non-conforming product is vital to prevent it from inadvertently entering the supply chain. Procedures must be documented to ensure any non-conforming product is:

- Identified
- Segregated from conforming product
- Prevented from further processing or release to a customer
- Disposed of and the details recorded.

## 4.13.2 Disposition of Non-Conforming Product

When product has been clearly identified as non-conforming, documentary procedures are required for detailing the disposition of such items. Tight control of non-conforming product is essential. There are a number of alternative methods for disposing of non-conforming product:

- Rework — then re-test to ensure it meets specification
- Regrade — for alternative applications

- Reject or scrap
- Return to the supplier if the problem is with purchased product
- Sell at a discounted price — providing the customer is fully advised of the quality status
- Release to the customer if he accepts the product after being notified of the problem
- Any reworked items must be subjected to rechecking as detailed in the inspection and test procedures
- The individual responsible for authorising the disposition of the non-conforming items must be named.

## Summary of Section 4.13

1. All non-conforming product must be identified and controlled.

2. Non-conforming items must be segregated and prevented from further processing or release to the customer. Use of a designated quarantine area is essential as a holding location for non-conforming items.

3. The disposition of non-conforming product must be determined and recorded and the individual responsible for these procedures named.

4. All aspects of non-conforming product must be recorded.

5. A choice of disposition alternatives is available and should be detailed in the Operational Procedures Manual.

6. When required by the contract a non-conforming item may be repaired by the supplier and if necessary a concession agreed with the customer, with a documented re-inspection undertaken.

# 4.14 CORRECTIVE AND PREVENTATIVE ACTION

## 4.14.1 General

When problems have been identified it is vitally important to take effective and documented action to prevent reoccurrences. Segregating non-conforming product is the initial step but it is essential to investigate the problem thoroughly to determine the underlying cause.

Corrective action therefore means identifying the problem and implementing changes in procedures to prevent them from being repeated. Details of corrective action must be recorded on a Non-Conformance Report — usually completed by departmental heads.

## 4.14.2 Corrective Action

Non-conformances that require corrective action arise from the following circumstances:

- Product, installation or service fault
- Supplier fails to fulfil exact purchase requirements
- Customer complaints
- Internal system or staff problems.

It is essential to identify the root cause of the problem and implement effective corrective action.

Corrective action is usually required for problems of a more serious nature or where a trend is developing and as such it is likely that the Quality Manager will liaise with one or more departmental heads to discuss remedial measures. Changes in operating procedures or documentation may be required in certain circumstances and such changes must be recorded.

### 4.14.3 Preventative Action

Generally a departmental head will initiate a Non-conformance Report to record a problem and will usually implement remedial action to prevent recurrence. All vital records, such as audit reports, customer complaints, quality records or service reports, may be used to initiate preventative procedures.

Remedial action must be analysed to ensure its long-term effectiveness and all actions taken must be discussed at a Management Review.

### Summary of Section 4.14

1.  Identify the non-conformance.

2.  Investigate the root cause of the problem.

3.  Initiate corrective action to prevent the problem reoccurring.

4.  Record the problem and corrective action details on a Non-Conformance Report.

5.  Serious problems and subsequent remedial action should be recorded on a Corrective Action Report following liaison between the Quality Manager and departmental heads.

6.  Monitor corrective action to ensure its ongoing effectiveness.

7.  Review all relevant operational and quality management documents to initiate preventative action procedures.

8.  Submit details of corrective and preventative actions for discussion and appraisal at a Management Review.

# 4.15 HANDLING, STORAGE, PACKAGING, PRESERVATION AND DELIVERY

### 4.15.1 General

Documented procedures must be established for the handling, storage, packaging, preservation and delivery of product.

### 4.15.2 Handling

Procedures are required to ensure that product is not damaged as it moves through the plant during processing or when moved from the production line to the storage area. Careful handling at all times is essential to prevent product damage or deterioration.

### 4.15.3 Storage

Designated storage areas or stock rooms must be secure and prevent damage or deterioration to product. This applies to items awaiting processing as well as those where production has been completed and are waiting despatch to a customer. Stock checks must be undertaken at designated intervals to assess product condition.

## 4.15.4 Packaging

Items of packaging such as cartons, bags and boxes must be stored in designated areas where they will not be subjected to damage or deterioration.

Packaged stock awaiting despatch must be clearly identified and packing line procedures must be controlled through documented procedures.

## 4.15.5 Preservation

Appropriate methods of product preservation must be implemented (such as cold storage or chilled storage) while product is under the supplier's control.

## 4.15.6 Delivery

Product must be protected during transportation to the customer and must be delivered in sound condition. Where third-party hauliers are used the same responsibility applies. This applies to the quality of all products following final inspection and test procedures.

Proof of delivery should be confirmed by issue of a Delivery Note, or a Collection Note when customers undertake their own collections.

## Summary of Section 4.15

1. All procedures relating to handling, storage, packaging, preservation and delivery of product must be formalised and supported by documentary controls.

2. Storage of finished product, packaging and raw materials must be secure and prevent damage and deterioration.

3. Packing line procedures and the movement of stock to and from the line to storage areas must be fully documented.

4.  Suitable product preservation facilities must be available.

5.  Product must arrive at the customer's premises in pristine condition.

6.  Documentation must control all deliveries and/or collections.

# 4.16 CONTROL OF QUALITY RECORDS

All records appertaining to the Quality System must be identified and stored together for ease of retrieval and reference. Records must be maintained for a minimum three-year period.

Quality Records are the primary evidence that the operational systems are working effectively and that customers' requirements are being totally satisfied. These records form an essential part of the accreditation process. They are the written proof of conformance to the Quality Assurance System - ISO 9000.

The following documents are essential to manage a Quality Assurance system. While they will vary according to individual company requirements the basic format will apply regardless of the type or size of the company implementing them. They are identified by a QA prefix, which means Quality Assurance, followed by a number. Examples of Quality Assurance documents are to be found in the Appendix.

## QA 01 — Quality Audit Schedule (Section 4.17)

The Quality Audit Schedule details dates and times of pre-planned internal audits (system checks).

## QA 01A — Quality Audit Checklist (Section 4.17)

Audits must be pre-planned and a series of relevant

questions recorded. The Quality Audit Checklist is used for recording questions and comments in each section of the organisation.

## QA 02 — Quality Audit Meeting Report (Section 4.17)

This form is used to present audit findings at Quality Audit Meetings and Management Reviews.

## QA 02A — Quality Audit Report (Section 4.17)

This is used to record information gathered during an internal audit — including observations for minor problems and non-conformances for major problems.

## QA 02B — Quality Audit Report (Summary) (Section 4.17)

This form highlights which sections of the Quality System have passed the audit and those which have been identified as non-conforming (N/C). Observations are also recorded.

Non-conforming sections must be re-audited when corrective action has been implemented.

## QA 03 — Non-Conformance Reports (Section 4.14)

These are completed by departmental heads when non-conformance arises — for example:

- Customer complaints
- System faults
- Non-conforming product identified
- Machine non-conformance
- Problems with supplier or supplier's product
- Staff/operative problems.

## QA 03A — Non-Conformance Register (Section 4.14)

This form is a summary sheet on which individual Non-Conformance Report details are recorded.

At a glance it can be determined which department or individual is causing problems, which suppliers fail to satisfy specific requirements most frequently and the origin of the customer complaints.

## QA 04 — Corrective Action Report (Section 4.14)

This is completed by the Quality Manager liaising with departmental heads when serious problems arise that may necessitate amending operating procedures.

## QA 05 — Suppliers' Non-Conformance Letter (Section 4.14)

When a supplier causes a serious problem a formal letter should be despatched to record the dissatisfaction and to issue a formal warning that further occurrences may result in the supplier being removed from the Approved Sub-Contractors' Register.

## QA 06 — Controlled Documents Issue Register (Section 4.5)

All internal documentation, data sheets, etc., and the name of their holders must be recorded on the Controlled Document Issue Register. All vital documentation essential for managing the business, including the Quality and Operational Procedures Manuals, should also be recorded. This includes documents and data from outside sources.

All document updates and amendments must also be recorded on this form.

## QA 07 — Quality/Operational Manual Amendment Control Form (Section 4.5)

Whenever changes to the Quality Manual or Operational Procedures Manual are made details are recorded on Form QA 07.

## QA 08 — Suppliers'/Subcontractors' Assessment Questionnaire (Section 4.6)

This questionnaire should be mailed to all major suppliers to determine their ISO 9000 accreditation status.

## QA 09 — Suppliers'/Subcontractors' Register (Section 4.6)

Suppliers' details are recorded on this Register when the completed questionnaires (QA 08) are returned.

## QA 10 — Training Record (Section 4.18)

This must be completed for every employee — including directors and management — and should record experience, qualifications and ISO 9000 training completed.

## QA 11 — Calibration Register (Section 4.11)

This records each item of inspection, measuring and test equipment and the date, nature and frequency of calibration tests to be undertaken.

## QA 12 — Customer Complaint Acknowledgement Letter (Section 4.14)

Following repeated or serious customer complaints a formal letter should be despatched indicating your intention to investigate and rectify the problem and advising the customer of the corrective action taken.

Forms QA 01-QA 12 are essential for controlling the Quality Assurance System. Additionally all companies will have their own internal documentation which should be used to control the vital stages or hold points throughout the organisation. The following are recommendations for consideration if they are not already in place — detailed by the appropriate section in the Standard. They will vary according to individual companies' procedures and sphere of operation and the following detail should be used only as a guide.

## Section 4.1 Quality System Requirements

No documents required.

## Section 4.2 Quality System

Documents QA 01-QA 12 are the vital documents to manage the Quality System.

## Section 4.3 Contract Review

- Enquiry sheet/register (costings can also be included on this form)
- Quotation sheet
- Sales order form (can be used to record amendments to customers' original orders)
- Invoice

## Section 4.4 Design Control

The design or drawing control sheet should incorporate:

- Updating record
- Statutory requirements
- Technical and organisational interfaces
- Reviews and design changes

- Design verification
- Design validation.

One control document may be adequate for many design projects but for larger, more complicated assignments a series of control documents will be required to ensure customers' exact requirements are satisfied on the completion of the design element of the contract.

## Section 4.5 Document and Data Control

QA 06 and QA 07.

## Section 4.6 Purchasing

- Purchase order form
- Purchase order register (if required).

## Section 4.7 Control of Customer-Supplied Product

A stock control record to ensure customer-supplied product is identified and stored separately.

## Section 4.8 Product Identification and Traceability

Stock records, warehousing and production controls to ensure purchased products are clearly identified and can be traced to their original supplier before, during production and while awaiting despatch to the customer.
    Production dates, machine and production line details, batch codes, etc., should be recorded by supervisors/managers to ensure all items are fully traceable.

## Section 4.9 Process Control

All checks undertaken at critical stages or hold points in

manufacturing of the process or installation must be recorded on control documentation and, through a signature, traceable to the individual responsible for completing the form.

## Section 4.10 Inspection and Testing

All inspection and test checks must be recorded:

- When suppliers' goods are initially received (receiving, inspecting and testing)

- During processing (in-process inspection and test)

- After processing, before release to the customer (final inspection and test).

## Section 4.11 Control of Inspection, Measuring and Test Equipment

QA 11.

## Section 4.12 Inspection and Test Status

All inspection and test records must be completed and retained as part of the company's Quality Records. These records include:

- Receiving inspection and test
- In-process
- Final inspection and test.

## Section 4.13 Control of Non-Conforming Product

Production or installation records. In some instances it may be necessary to complete a Non-conformance Report — QA 03.

## Section 4.14 Corrective and Preventative Action

QA 03 and QA 04.

## Section 4.15 Handling, Storage, Packaging, Preservation and Delivery

- Record details of product leaving the production line for storage in the warehouse
- Record details of product moved to and from packing lines
- Stock records of packaging held must be maintained
- Stock levels of product and packaging must be commensurate with sales
- Proof of delivery or collection is required.

## Section 4.16 Control of Quality Records

Quality Records are deemed to be all documents described in this section and must be retained for a minimum three-year period before disposal.

## Section 4.17 Internal Quality Audits

QA 01 — QA 02B.

## Section 4.18 Training

QA 10.

## Section 4.19 Servicing

Service Record Card.

## Section 4.20 Statistical Techniques

Statistical or performance record sheet (if applicable).

## Summary of Section 4.16

1.  All Quality Records must be easily retrievable and maintained for three years before disposal.

2.  All Quality Management documents QA 01 — QA 12 should be implemented to ensure the efficient operation and control of the Quality System.

3.  Maintain a file for each Quality Record.

4.  Alter and amend the documents detailed in the Appendix to suit individual company requirements.

5.  These are the primary documentary records that will be checked by the accreditation body. Complete them with care.

6.  All documents must be signed and dated.

7.  Every organisation will complete its own internal control documentation and all items must be dated and signed and will be reviewed by the accreditation body during the assessment process.

# 4.17 INTERNAL QUALITY AUDITS

Internal audits using documents QA 01 — QA 02B are the essential records for ensuring the Quality System is working efficiently.

At least one internal auditor should be appointed (auditing a department for which an individual has responsibility is not permitted). Most organisations appoint two internal auditors. At least one internal audit per year must be completed and recorded. It is recommended that six-monthly audits are implemented so that any problems arising can be identified reasonably quickly and corrective action implemented.

Audit results should be discussed with all relevant staff and departmental management at a Management Review.

Where non-conformances are identified at audit remedial action must be implemented and re-audited to ensure its effectiveness at a later date.

## Summary of Section 4.17

1. Initiate a system for internal audits.

2. Appoint one or two internal auditors.

3. Undertake at least two audits per year.

4. Document audit findings and discuss them with relevant members of staff at a Management Review.

# 4.18 TRAINING

The Company must maintain a Training Record for each member of staff and record:

- All previous training and experience
- Future training requirements.

A well-managed company must ensure its workforce receive adequate training to improve working practices, efficiency and operative skills and knowledge.

Ongoing training in Quality Assurance is essential. All personnel performing specific tasks must be adequately trained. Training must be continuous and must be undertaken by every employee to ensure the operational effectiveness of the Quality Assurance System.

## Summary of Section 4.18

1. Maintain Training Records for all staff.

2. Pre-plan future training requirements.

3. Training in Quality Assurance is vital for everyone.

# 4.19 SERVICING

Where servicing is a specific requirement of the contract or order the supplier must maintain documented procedures for:

- Undertaking the necessary servicing requirements
- Checking and reporting that the servicing undertaken meets the specified requirements.

## Summary of Section 4.19

1. All servicing requirements must be pre-planned and documented.

2. The nature of any servicing must be recorded together with checks and reporting procedures to ensure the work completed satisfies specified requirements.

# 4.20 STATISTICAL TECHNIQUES

## 4.20.1 Identification of Need

Statistical techniques can be used in a wide variety of ways, i.e.

- Processing capability
- Machine performance
- Shift performance
- Rejection levels
- Product characteristics.

## 4.20.2 Procedures

While many forms of statistical analysis are generally more applicable to large organisations, smaller firms can also benefit by using Non-conformance Reports as a performance indicator to measure departmental efficiency.

Where necessary procedures should be implemented to control the application of statistical techniques identified in 4.20.1.

## Summary of Section 4.20

1. Implement statistical techniques that will provide vital performance information.

2. Give careful consideration to methods of statistical analysis that will provide useful information.

3. Use Non-Conformance Reports as a performance indicator.

# SECTION 5

# PREPARING QUALITY ASSURANCE MANUALS

# PREPARING QUALITY ASSURANCE MANUALS

The implementation of ISO 9000 is based on two manuals:

- The Quality Policy Manual
- The Operational Procedures Manual

and the supporting documentation which effectively controls the system, i.e. Quality Assurance documents and individual companies' internal control documents.

Manuals should be written in simplistic and concise terms so that every member of the staff can understand them. Documents should also be clear, uncomplicated and straightforward to complete.

## What is the Start Point for Preparing a Manual?

### The Quality Manual

Before a Quality Manual can be written it is essential to obtain a copy of the International Standard ISO 9000 1994, available from:

British Standards Institution
2 Park Street
London
W1A 2BS

British Standards Institution
Linford Wood
Milton Keynes
MK14 6LE

or it can be ordered through any good bookshop.

The Standard is divided into 20 elements; each one will form a specific section in the Quality Policy Manual.

The terminology of the International Standard effectively describes what the company must do to conform to the requirements in each of the 20 sections, i.e.

- The supplier will establish and maintain documented procedures through the company
- The supplier will plan and control all aspects of production
- The supplier will assess all subcontractors.

Writing a basic Quality Manual need be no more than a rehash of the Standard tailored to suit individual company requirements, except that where the Standard tells the reader what the company (supplier) must do the language should be slightly altered to read 'The Company'. In other words, the Quality Policy Manual is an account of what an organisation does to satisfy each of the 20 sections of the International Standard.

The Quality Manual is a policy statement. How individual companies interpret and control the 20 elements of the International Standard ISO 9000 must be defined in the Operational Procedures Manual.

There is no mandatory requirement to number the pages but each page must be headed 'Quality Policy Manual'. The bottom of each page must include the following detail (an example is provided in the Appendix):

Authorised signature:    Issue:

Date:    Revision:

## The Operational Procedures Manual

The same 20 sections of the International Standard ISO 9000 apply to the preparation of the Operational Procedures Manual.

The Quality Manual describes what an organisation does to satisfy the requirements of the 20 elements of the Standard; the Operational Procedures Manual describes how it is done with reference to the control documents completed in each section.

For each of the 20 points it is essential that working practices and controlling documentation are recorded in the manual and that they fully satisfy all the essential requirements of the International Standard ISO 9000. Where a section or part of a section does not apply to an individual company, confirm this with a statement in the Operational Procedures Manual: 'This section has been addressed but is not applicable.'

- Use bullet points whenever possible
- Do not get bogged down with too much detail
- Ensure all relevant procedures are recorded
- Use simple language so all members of staff are able to understand it
- Record each control document used by name and identification number whenever the written procedures require it to be mentioned.

Page numbers are not required in the Operational Procedures Manual but each page must be headed with the title of the section, the reference number determined by the International Standard and the number of pages in the section — for example, Purchasing 4.6, Page 1 of 6.

At the bottom of each page the following must appear (an example is provided in the Appendix):

Authorised signature:    Issue:

Date:    Revision:

## Documentation

There are two sets of documentation in every organisation implementing a Quality Assurance System:

- The Quality Management documents which control the Quality System (QA 01 — QA 12)
- The organisation's own internal documents/registers which control all relevant operating procedures.

The Quality Management documents QA 01-QA 12 have already been described and each is identified by its own number and name. A similar policy of naming and numbering all internal documents used to control the important sections of the organisation that are essential for conformity to the International Standard must be recorded. For example, the purchase order form used by Richard Smith and Co. will be identified as RS 1.

When preparing an Operational Procedures Manual reference must be made in the text, when relevant, to the document used in each section of the Standard. For example, under Section 4.6 (Purchasing), when describing how purchases are confirmed, reference will be made to the Purchase Order Form.

Before the Quality and Operational Procedures Manuals are written, ensure the International Standard ISO 9000 has been understood and all relevant sections of the Standard included in the text.

Whenever the Standard states 'procedures must be established' or 'document and maintain procedures' then this is exactly what every organisation must do. If there is no procedure or a document in place where required by the Standard then they must be originated and implemented.

Careful preparation of the Manuals is essential — they are the documentary evidence that a Quality Assurance System has been implemented and adequately controlled. They detail the procedures that must be followed and the documents that must be completed. Examples of all Quality Management documentation (QA 01-QA 12) and relevant internal control documentation must be included in an appendix at the back of the Operational Procedures Manual.

# SECTION 6

## HOW A CONSULTANT CAN HELP

# HOW A CONSULTANT CAN HELP

There is nothing to prevent any company preparing its own Quality Policy and Operational Procedures Manuals providing sufficient ongoing time can be allocated and the exact requirements of the Standard are fulfilled. It is common for consultants to be retained to:

- Write the Manuals
- Check the systems for conformity against the Standard
- Implement Quality Assurance and Operational Procedures
- Ensure documentation is fit for the purpose
- Train staff (particularly the Quality Manager)
- Undertake initial internal audits
- Monitor progress
- Assist the company to final accreditation.

Experienced consultants have the expertise to ensure Quality Assurance projects are completed to the satisfaction of the accreditation body and that everyone in the company fully understands what is required to operate a successful and meaningful Quality Assurance System. Consultants have the time to dedicate to a project to ensure it does not drag on for an inordinate length of time and are always available for future help and guidance. Naturally there is a cost factor when consultants are retained, but this can be insignificant if the project is completed quickly, professionally and the company achieves a successful accreditation first time.

Select your consultant with care. There are a great number who claim to have expertise but have only a hazy knowledge of what is required to satisfy all the requirements of the Standard. Some produce Manuals that are too complicated and unwieldy, some are extremely overpriced, and some fail to offer an adequate back-up service. Check the consultant's credentials, question the level of expertise and take out references. Getting Quality Assurance right first time is essential. Failure to retain a suitable consultant can be costly.

Consultants are the backbone of Quality Assurance implementation and can provide a great deal of invaluable assistance. It is not always necessary to retain them to undertake all the work; they can assist the client purely in an advisory capacity and fees will be proportionately lower.

It is not always necessary for the consultant to have specific industry sector knowledge. Understanding the International Standard is the vital prerequisite.

The average consultancy fee should be in the range of £340-£650 per day and for most small to medium-sized organisations no more than 15 days will be required to complete a full implementation project.

# SECTION 7

## THE IMPLICATIONS FOR EVERY BUSINESS

# THE IMPLICATIONS FOR EVERY BUSINESS

## Costs

The vast majority of companies, because they are not large organisations, do not require a full-time Quality Assurance Manager. The Quality Assurance Manager's role will be undertaken by an executive already working in the business and this may well be the Production Manager, Operations Manager or the Works Manager.

For companies using their own staff to prepare the Manuals and not retaining a consultant, costs can be reduced — providing they 'get it right'. Many organisations implementing ISO 9000 for themselves frequently take an inordinate length of time to achieve a satisfactory system and often fail to understand fully all that is required for a successful accreditation.

### Consultant's And Accreditation Fees

- Consultant's fees to complete the total project: £4800-8000.
- Accreditation body fees: £1200-2000, according to the size of the organisation seeking assessment.
- Thereafter the accreditation body will levy a surveillance charge for inspecting the systems once or twice per year. This fee is negotiable but will be approximately £850-1500.

- There may be some additional small costs for new document printing and photocopying but this will be minimal.

## Staff

Every member of staff has a vital part to play in the successful implementation and maintenance of a Quality Assurance System. Their function is to perform their duties exactly as they are defined in the Operational Procedures Manual and to ensure that at all times Quality Assurance is their major priority.

A Quality Assurance Manager must be appointed together with one or two Internal Auditors, but for most organisations these are not full-time roles although it is vital that appropriate amounts of time are dedicated to ISO 9000. Systems do not run themselves — they have to be managed, monitored and when necessary altered and amended to achieve the desired end results.

The Quality Manager, working in tandem with departmental heads and directors, is responsible for the day-to-day control of all Quality Assurance Matters.

Time must be allocated to 'Management Reviews' — meetings where all Quality Assurance issues are discussed. It is advisable to hold monthly Management Reviews to ensure the smooth running of the system and to correct quickly any non-conformances that have been identified.

## Time

For the majority of organisations, while Quality Assurance is an ongoing function operating throughout the company, it is unusual for excessive amounts of time to be required to oversee the system once it is up and running efficiently. The Quality Manager will most probably have his other duties to attend to and it is unlikely that ISO 9000 matters will take up more than a few (4-5) hours each week. Much will depend on the effectiveness of the system, the control and correction of non-conformances and the competence of all staff to interpret and implement Quality Assurance functions.

# SECTION 8

## THE BENEFITS FOR EVERY BUSINESS

# THE BENEFITS FOR EVERY BUSINESS

ISO 9000 unquestionably brings significant benefits to organisations when a sound and easily manageable Quality Assurance system has been implemented. The primary benefits are:

- Reduction in costs through increased efficiency and the elimination of errors and waste. This is achievable through a series of documented checks and controls at every vital stage of the company which will minimise potentially costly errors and may lead to credibility problems with customers.

- Sound working practices, instructions and documentation are detailed in the Quality Policy and Operational Procedures Manuals — so managing and controlling the business becomes easier. Everyone in the organisation knows what to do and how to do it.

- Best working practice prevents 'fire-fighting' and enables the company to operate efficiently.

- Increased efficiency reduces the cost base and enables companies to become increasingly competitive.

- ISO 9000 ensures a policy of continuous personnel and systems improvement.

- Sales potential is significantly increased when customers appreciate that ISO 9000 means a 'right first time' approach.

- The Standard is accepted world-wide, which is vital for companies seeking to export their products.

- The ability to supply larger companies or those organisations who insist all their suppliers of goods and services must be accredited ISO 9000 companies.

- Without ISO 9000 it is becoming increasingly difficult to secure registration on tendering lists.

- Quality Assurance invokes a strong team spirit — everyone has to pull in the same direction to achieve the best end result and a sense of pride runs through companies that have achieved a successful accreditation.

- ISO 9000 is an excellent marketing tool — without it many companies' future survival may be jeopardised. It is a sound investment in the future.

- Even in the darkest days of the recession, when business failures reached previously unheard of levels, only a minute number of failures were ISO 9000 accredited companies. Because Quality Assured companies are controlled and managed efficiently their chances of failing are greatly reduced.

- ISO 9000 provides the 'edge' over competing companies who do not have a Quality Assurance System and enables them to develop a position of strength from which to negotiate future contracts.

# SECTION 9

## STAFF TRAINING

# STAFF TRAINING

All staff must be made aware at the earliest possible moment of the company's intention to seek ISO 9000 accreditation. A sound Quality Assurance system can function effectively only if all the staff understand the ethos of Quality Assurance and appreciate that their individual and collective responsibilities are essential for the operational procedures to work effectively for the benefit of the company and its customers.

Regular induction meetings should be held for short periods with staff attending in small groups on a departmental basis. Small groups are preferable because they encourage questions and comments that are unlikely to be forthcoming in larger groups.

Ongoing staff training is essential if everyone in the company is to have a sound understanding of Quality issues. It is equally important to encourage comments and opinions from staff — they can have an extremely useful and positive influence on Quality Assurance. All training sessions should be detailed on individual Training Records which form part of the Quality System.

# SECTION 10

## AUDITING TECHNIQUES

# AUDITING TECHNIQUES

Internal Quality System Audits must be completed fully and documented at least once each year and before final accreditation can be achieved. They must also be undertaken at least annually by trained and competent internal auditors in the years following successful accreditation.

Accreditation is a third-party audit: internal audits are usually conducted by the company's own staff and are vital for checking the Quality System is operating effectively and for highlighting deficiencies that will require corrective action. A systemised approach to internal auditing is essential and the Quality Management Forms QA 01-QA02B are the audit control and appraisal documents which should be completed by the appointed auditor(s).

Increasingly, accreditation bodies are seeking detailed documentary proof that in-depth audits have been undertaken and the results recorded and analysed and, where necessary, improvements to the system implemented.

- Only use trained personnel to undertake internal audits
    - individuals who are familiar with the Quality Assurance System
    - have good communication skills and the ability to deal with staff at all levels.

- Before an audit, checklists and pertinent questions should be prepared to enable a detailed investigation into
  — each department's operating procedures and controls
  — the effectiveness of each section of the Quality Policy and Operational Procedures Manuals.

- Pre-plan an audit timetable by department or by individual section of the Manuals. Small companies will be able to complete an audit in one or two days; larger organisations may conclude an audit over several weeks or months.

- The basis of the audit is to
  — Ask relevant questions in each department — for example:
    'Tell me how you undertake your job'
    'Show me the documents you complete'
    'What happens when a non-conformance arises?'
  — Audit trails are also essential. Follow a document or form around the company from the department or individual who initiates it until its usefulness is concluded and it is filed.
  — Check working documents are completed correctly, dated, signed off and therefore traceable to an individual.
  — Ensure departmental heads are advised of non-conformances and the reasons for them.
  — Advise all staff of the need to complete internal audits.
  — Each audit should be followed by a Management Review (Quality Assurance meeting) to discuss the findings in detail and where necessary agree remedial action to correct non-conformances. The Management Review findings should be retained and minutes circulated to all departmental heads and supervisors.

Audits are an integral and vital element of a Quality Assurance System and the fact that they are undertaken infrequently must not undermine their importance. Audits are one of the primary methods for identifying weaknesses that could threaten the efficiency of the Quality Assurance System.

# SECTION 11

## DISPELLING THE MISCONCEPTIONS, MISUNDERSTANDINGS AND MISAPPREHENSIONS OF ISO 9000

# DISPELLING THE MISCONCEPTIONS, MISUNDERSTANDINGS AND MISAPPREHENSIONS OF ISO 9000

## Will Consultants Tell me How to Run my Business?

There seems to be a general misconception when a consultant is retained to complete an ISO 9000 project that he will change the company's entire operating procedures. Not so.

The consultant's role is to conduct an Internal Audit to evaluate what systems and documentation are already in place. He will then compare the company's current procedures with the requirements of the International Standard. Where systems or documentary deficiencies are identified the consultant will, by liaison with the client company, present options that will ensure compliance with the Standard.

Equally, it is not the role of the accreditation body to dictate to the company how it must operate. In fact, by documenting its procedures the company is advising the accreditation body how its operational and documentary controls function. The company therefore advises the accreditation body, through its procedural manual, how it operates. Providing full compliance with the requirements of the Standard can be proven to the accreditation body then a successful assessment will be achieved.

Companies can work to any set of procedures that

best suit them operationally. If before seeking final accreditation they are embracing the ethos of Quality Assurance and are satisfying all relevant elements of the International Standard, it is not the role of the consultant or the accreditation body to implement change for the sake of change.

## Accreditation Takes Years to Achieve

There are numerous examples of companies taking in excess of two years to reach readiness for final accreditation. Such lengthy periods of time are not necessary if sufficient dedicated time is allocated to ISO 9000 progression on an ongoing basis. For most organisations, other than the very largest, the following timescale is practical.

### 12-16 Weeks

- Undertake initial systems audit
- Complete Quality Assurance and Operational Procedures Manuals
- Review and amendment of control documentation
- Train staff, including Quality Manager
- Full implementation of Quality System.

It is usual for a consultant to be retained if full implementation is to be satisfactorily completed in a four-month period.

An additional 3-4 month period is required to ensure the Quality System is working and to amend and improve procedures and/or documentation where problems have been identified. At that stage an initial internal audit should be completed and fully documented and again, if there are no major non-conformances identified, then is the appropriate time to apply to an accreditation body.

# Accreditation Bodies Undertake Spot Checks

Accreditation bodies do not just 'drop in': they visit companies by appointment to undertake final assessment. The accreditation process is usually in two parts.

## Document Assessment

The Manuals and all supporting documentation are reviewed by the accreditation body to ensure they fulfil the requirements of the International Standard.

If the accreditation body are not completely satisfied with the Manuals at Document Assessment they will recommend amendments.

## Final Assessment

The accreditation body visit the organisation seeking assessment, by appointment, and check that the company's systems and documentation are working satisfactorily and all aspects of the Standard are in place.

## Implementing ISO 9000 Is Very Expensive

There are many stories of the high cost of implementing ISO 9000 but most are out of proportion with reality.

Full implementation costs for a small business could be in the region of £2,000-3,000. For medium-size organisations the costs should be £3,000-5,000. The costs for larger or multi-branch organisations will be proportionately higher but should not exceed £8,000-10,000. In addition to implementation costs there will be an accreditation fee, which is initially paid on final assessment with a slightly reduced fee payable each year for surveillance visits.

## ISO 9000 Is Too Unwieldy Because of the Additional Paperwork

It is a fact that some additional paperwork is required to control a Quality Assurance System. However, this should be minimal for most organisations and ideally simple to complete. There is no merit in introducing overcomplicated operating systems and control documents. Without documentary controls it is impossible to maintain an efficient Quality Assurance System and there would be no evidence for the accreditation bodies to inspect during Final Assessment.

## ISO 9000 Is Difficult to Understand

Quality Assurance is little more than commercial common sense and the application of reliable procedures to ensure the customer's exact requirements are constantly satisfied. Individual company managers are the experts in their own sphere of operation and Quality Assurance merely enhances this expertise through the implementation of documented procedures. There is nothing complicated or difficult to understand once the ethos of Quality Assurance is appreciated.

## ISO 9000 Is Only Suitable for Large Organisations

Not true. Even the smallest business can benefit from implementing Quality Assurance and reduce costs through the minimising of potentially costly errors. For all companies Quality Assurance is an invaluable marketing tool and should be viewed as a sound investment in the future. Initial implementation costs can be quickly recouped by the resultant efficiencies that emanate from sound operating practices.

## Footnote

I hope this handbook has presented a detailed yet practical insight into ISO 9000-Quality Assurance and perhaps removed any fears and misconceptions. I have avoided using jargon and "buzz" words and I have attempted to present what for many appears to be a complicated and difficult subject in simple terms that can be easily understood.

Quality Assurance is the positive way forward and I can think of few, if any, organisations that would not benefit from the implementation of ISO 9000.

John Shaw

# APPENDIX

## DOCUMENTS FOR MANAGING A QUALITY ASSURANCE SYSTEM

# QUALITY MANAGEMENT
# DOCUMENTATION

The following pages give examples of:

QA 01    Quality Audit Schedule
QA 01A   Quality Audit Checklist
QA 02    Quality Audit Meeting Report
QA 02A   Quality Audit Report
QA 02B   Quality Audit Report (Summary)
QA 03    Non-Conformance Report
QA 03A   Non-Conformance Register
QA 04    Corrective Action Report
QA 05    Suppliers' Non-Conformance Letter
QA 06    Controlled Documents Issue Register
QA 07    Quality/Operational Manual Amendment Control Form
QA 08    Suppliers'/Sub-Contractors' Questionnaire
QA 09    Suppliers'/Sub-Contractors' Register
QA 10    Training Record
QA 11    Calibration Register
QA 12    Customer Complaint Acknowledgement Letter
Quality Policy Manual — sample page
Operational Procedures Manual — sample page

# Quality Audit Schedule

| Department/Activity audited | | J | F | M | A | M | J | J | A | S | O | N | D |
|---|---|---|---|---|---|---|---|---|---|---|---|---|---|
| Management Responsibilities | 4.1 | | | | | | | | | | | | |
| Quality System | 4.2 | | | | | | | | | | | | |
| Contract Review | 4.3 | | | | | | | | | | | | |
| Design Control | 4.4 | | | | | | | | | | | | |
| Document and Data Control | 4.5 | | | | | | | | | | | | |
| Purchasing | 4.6 | | | | | | | | | | | | |
| Control of Customer-Supplied Product | 4.7 | | | | | | | | | | | | |
| Product Identification and Traceability | 4.8 | | | | | | | | | | | | |
| Process Control | 4.9 | | | | | | | | | | | | |
| Inspection and Testing | 4.10 | | | | | | | | | | | | |
| Control of Inspection, Measuring and Test Equipment | 4.11 | | | | | | | | | | | | |
| Inspection and Test Status | 4.12 | | | | | | | | | | | | |
| Control of Non-conforming Product | 4.13 | | | | | | | | | | | | |
| Corrective and Preventative Action | 4.14 | | | | | | | | | | | | |
| Handling, Storage, Packaging, Preservation and Delivery | 4.15 | | | | | | | | | | | | |
| Control of Quality Records | 4.16 | | | | | | | | | | | | |
| Internal Quality Audits | 4.17 | | | | | | | | | | | | |
| Training | 4.18 | | | | | | | | | | | | |
| Servicing | 4.19 | | | | | | | | | | | | |
| Statistical Technique | 4.20 | | | | | | | | | | | | |

Code

Clear space means System OK

Shaded area means System Deficient

Audit Number

# Quality Audit Checklist

| Ref | Question | Y | N | Comment |
|---|---|---|---|---|
|  |  |  |  |  |
|  |  |  |  |  |
|  |  |  |  |  |
|  |  |  |  |  |
|  |  |  |  |  |
|  |  |  |  |  |
|  |  |  |  |  |
|  |  |  |  |  |
|  |  |  |  |  |
|  |  |  |  |  |
|  |  |  |  |  |
|  |  |  |  |  |
|  |  |  |  |  |
|  |  |  |  |  |
|  |  |  |  |  |
|  |  |  |  |  |
|  |  |  |  |  |
|  |  |  |  |  |
|  |  |  |  |  |
|  |  |  |  |  |
|  |  |  |  |  |
|  |  |  |  |  |
|  |  |  |  |  |
|  |  |  |  |  |

# Quality Audit Meeting Report

| Audit Report No: | Date: | Auditor(s): | Department Audited: |
|---|---|---|---|
| Type of Audit | Procedure: | Checklist Ref: | Department Head: |

Opening meeting:

Closing meeting:

Re-Audit date agreed as:

| NCR's | C.A.R. | Observation |
|---|---|---|

Agreed by Department Head:

Print name:

Signature:

Audit complete:

# Quality Audit Report

Auditor: .................

Date: .................

| | No. | Page......of...... |
|---|---|---|

| ISO Ref. | Page No. | | NC / 0 |
|---|---|---|---|
| | | | |
| | | | |
| | | | |
| | | | |
| | | | |
| | | | |
| | | | |
| | | | |
| | | | |
| | | | |
| | | | |
| | | | |
| | | | |

SPECIMEN

# Quality Audit Report (Summary)

QA 02B

Date: ...................................

Auditor: ...............................

| Ref. | Dept. | Procedure | Yes | N/C | OBS |
|------|-------|-----------|-----|-----|-----|
| 4.1 | | Management Responsibilities | | | |
| 4.2 | Q | Quality System | | | |
| 4.3 | S | Contract Review | | | |
| 4.4 | | Design Control | | | |
| 4.5 | Q | Document and Data Control | | | |
| 4.6 | A | Purchasing | | | |
| 4.7 | | Control of Customer-Supplied Product | | | |
| 4.8 | W | Product Identification and Traceability | | | |
| 4.9 | W | Process Control | | | |
| 4.10 | W | Inspection and Testing | | | |
| 4.11 | Q | Control of Inspection, Measuring and Test Equipment | | | |
| 4.12 | W | Inspection and Test Status | | | |
| 4.13 | Q | Control of Non-Conforming Product | | | |
| 4.14 | Q | Corrective and Preventative Action | | | |
| 4.15 | | Handling, Storage, Packaging, Preservation and Delivery | | | |
| 4.16 | Q | Control of Quality Records | | | |
| 4.17 | Q | Internal Quality Audits | | | |
| 4.18 | Q | Training | | | |
| 4.19 | | Servicing | | | |
| 4.20 | | Statistical Techniques | | | |

S = Sales       A = Administration

W = Works (Process)   Q = Quality

133

# Non-Conformance Report    QA 03

| | | | ISO Ref | QM Page |
|---|---|---|---|---|
| No: | Date: | | Non-conformance | |
| Non-conforming Dept | Head: | | Observation | |
| Originating Dept | Head: | | Customer complaints | |

| Non-conformance | | Customer | | Job No. | |
|---|---|---|---|---|---|
| Operative | | Name | Trade/Activity | | |
| Machine | | Ident/Description | | | |
| Supplier | | Name | Location | Haulier | |
| | | PO No.    Date    DN    No.    Date | | | |
| Customer Complaint | | Name<br><br>Address | | | |

Originated by:                    Signature:

Action taken by:                    Signature:        Date:

| | | | | |
|---|---|---|---|---|
| Action: Department Head | ✔ | Closed out | Action: Quality   Manager | ✔ |
| Quality Manager | | By: | QA 04 Completed           No. | |
| Re-worktime/Concession | Cost | | QA 09 Amend Supplier Records | |
| | | | QA 11 Amend Calibration Register | |
| | | Date: | P&E Records | |
| | | | Operative | |
| | | | | |
| | | | | |
| Total | | | | |

134

# Non-Conformance Register

| Non-Conformance | | | | | | | | Customer complaint | | Type | | | |
|---|---|---|---|---|---|---|---|---|---|---|---|---|---|
| No. | Date | Non-Conforming Department | Originating Department | Customer | Our Operative/ Machine/Site | Supplier | ISO Ref. QA 04 | Name | Cost of N/C | N/C | OBS | CC | Close Out |
| | | | | | | | | | | | | | |
| | | | | | | | | | | | | | |
| | | | | | | | | | | | | | |
| | | | | | | | | | | | | | |
| | | | | | | | | | | | | | |
| | | | | | | | | | | | | | |
| | | | | | | | | | | | | | |
| | | | | | | | | | | | | | |
| | | | | | | | | | | | | | |
| | | | | | | | | | | | | | |
| | | | | | | | | | | | | | |
| | | | | | | | | | | | | | |
| | | | | | | | | | | | | | |
| | | | | | | | | | | | | | |

135

# Corrective Action Report

QA 04

No: ........................

Date: ........................

| |
|---|
| Date |
| Department |
| QA 03/03 A Reference |
| Other identification sources |
| Operative/Supplier (Site/Equipment) |
| Report (use reverse side, if necessary) |
| Action taken by ................................................................ (use reverse side if necessary) |
| Re-Audit (state date planned) |
| Comments |

Report must be numbered sequentially

Three copies  – Top copy Department Head/Supplier as relevant

          – 2nd copy Managing Director

          – 3rd copy Quality Manager

# Supplier's Non-Conformance letter QA 05

Dear Sirs

Please note an error on your Delivery Note ......................
dated ............. referring to our Purchase Order ...................
dated ..................., details of which appear on our Non-Conformance
Report No.....................

All instances of incorrect deliveries are noted in our Supplier's
Register and, upon review, may jeopardise your Approved Supplier
Status with our Company.

137

# Controlled Documents Issue Register

QA 06

| Issue date | Title/Description | Date/Other reference | Issue No. | Replaces Issue No. | Holder/Number | Disposition of old issue |
|---|---|---|---|---|---|---|
| | | | | | | |
| | | | | | | |
| | | | | | | |
| | | | | | | |
| | | | | | | |
| | | | | | | |
| | | | | | | |
| | | | | | | |
| | | | | | | |
| | | | | | | |
| | | | | | | |
| | | | | | | |

SPECIMEN

138

# Quality/Operational Manual Amendment Control Form

| Issue | | | | Replaces | | | | Reason for amendment | Control copies sent |
|---|---|---|---|---|---|---|---|---|---|
| Date issued | Section No. | Page | Revision | Date issued | Section No. | Page | Revision | | |
| | | | | | | | | | |
| | | | | | | | | | |
| | | | | | | | | | |
| | | | | | | | | | |
| | | | | | | | | | |
| | | | | | | | | | |
| | | | | | | | | | |
| | | | | | | | | | |
| | | | | | | | | | |
| | | | | | | | | | |
| | | | | | | | | | |
| | | | | | | | | | |

Dear Sirs

In our quest to ensure our clients receive the best possible service and response to their needs we have decided as a company to embrace the ethos of ISO 9000. In order to achieve our goal we require your help with the following information regarding your company.

1. Full company name:..............................................................
   Address: ........................................................................
   ...................................................................................
   ...................................................................................
   Postcode ......................................

2. Type of product or service:..................................................
   ...................................................................................

3. Who is responsibility for Quality Assurance?
   ...................................................................................
   Position: .......................................................................
   Telephone: ..............................  Fax: ...............................

4. Are you registered with any QA Approved Body?  Yes/No
   If so, which?....................................................................
   Scope of Registration:.......................................................

If you hold a Quality Assurance Certificate will you please forward a copy of your Registration Certificate.

Thank you for your assistance.

# Supplier's/Subcontractor's Register

| QA 08 | Name | Location | Type of product or service | Performance (QA 03/Date) | | | | Status Review |
|---|---|---|---|---|---|---|---|---|
| Assess Code | | | | QA 03/Date | QA 03/Date | QA 03/Date | QA 03/Date | QA 04 |
| | | | | | | | | |
| | | | | | | | | |
| | | | | | | | | |
| | | | | | | | | |
| | | | | | | | | |
| | | | | | | | | |
| | | | | | | | | |
| | | | | | | | | |
| | | | | | | | | |
| | | | | | | | | |
| | | | | | | | | |

| Employee's name: | | Title: | |
|---|---|---|---|
| Age: | | Dept.: | |
| Employment commenced: | | | |
| Qualifications: | | | |
| Previous training: | | | |
| | Date | Observations | |
| Initial training use of QS | | | |

| Other training agreed |
|---|
| |
| |
| |
| |
| |
| |
| |
| |
| |
| |
| |

| Next review | | | | |
|---|---|---|---|---|

# Calibration Register

Year:

| Ident No. | Serial No. | Description | Test Freq | Auth. | Tolerances | Test Refs | Date | Y/N | QA 03 | Retest Date | Test Refs | Date | Y/N | QA 03 | Retest Date |
|-----------|-----------|-------------|-----------|-------|------------|-----------|------|-----|-------|-------------|-----------|------|-----|-------|-------------|
| | | | | | | | | | | | | | | | |
| | | | | | | | | | | | | | | | |
| | | | | | | | | | | | | | | | |
| | | | | | | | | | | | | | | | |
| | | | | | | | | | | | | | | | |
| | | | | | | | | | | | | | | | |
| | | | | | | | | | | | | | | | |
| | | | | | | | | | | | | | | | |
| | | | | | | | | | | | | | | | |
| | | | | | | | | | | | | | | | |
| | | | | | | | | | | | | | | | |
| | | | | | | | | | | | | | | | |
| | | | | | | | | | | | | | | | |
| | | | | | | | | | | | | | | | |

143

# Customer Complaint Acknowledgement Letter

Dear Sirs

We have noted the comments of your letter dated/telephone call today and express our concern at any inconvenience this may have caused.

In addition to any immediate remedial action we have taken, your comments will be fully investigated by our Quality Manager, who will make a further report to you and, if necessary, amend our Quality Systems.

Assuring you of our best attention at all times.

# Title: Management Responsibilities

# INDEX

# Index

# The Quality Revolution
## Best Practice from the World's Leading Companies
### Steve Smith

*(HC, £19.95, 400pp, 234 x 156mm, 1-85251-113-3)*

Total Quality has caused one of the biggest shake-ups ever in western management practice. Today, Quality in business is a prerequisite for success. *The Quality Revolution* looks at how successful companies have transformed their businesses with Quality and how they have obtained major benefits as a result.

*The Quality Revolution* identifies lessons for all managers. Anyone with vision and determination can lead their own Quality revolution. *The Quality Revolution* shows how.

Steve Smith has been learning about revolutionary change for twenty years. In that time he has helped over a hundred and fifty organisations, including many blue chip names, to manage change more effectively and positively. He is chairman of Quest Quality, an international management consultancy which focuses on transforming organisations.

Dr Smith is one of the pioneers of the Quality movement in Europe. Before forming Quest Quality in 1988, he was a director of PA Consulting Services, where he set up the TQM division in the early '80s. Prior to that he was a lecturer at the University of Aston in Birmingham for two years and a manager with Chrysler for eight years.

**'Books about TQM and quality have poured out of publishers in recent years. But few are as practical or valuable as *The Quality Revolution*. This book is packed with the kind of hands-on detail which brings a quality programme to life.'**
*Executive Management*

# Guides to W Edwards Deming's Quality Theories

W Edwards Deming was arguably the founder of Total Quality Management. His pioneering approach first came into public acclaim when he was employed by the Japanese to assist in their corporate reconstruction following the Second World War. Honoured by the Japanese for his remarkable success, Deming went on to become the recognised master of Quality.

Management Books 2000 publishes a unique collection of guides to Deming's theories and principles, as set out below.

## The Deming Management Method
### Mary Walton
*(HB, £16.95, PB, £9.99, 256pp, 234mm x 156mm)*

The definitive basic guide, reprinted several times since publication in1989. Recommended by the British Deming Association as an introduction to the Deming's theories and principles.

**'Lucid, practical and thoroughly convincing'** *Business*

## Deming Management At Work
### Mary Walton
*(HB, £16.95, 256pp, 234mm x 156mm)*

A companion volume to *The Deming Management Method* this book is a review of Deming's theory *in practice*, taking a detailed look at six successful companies which have followed the Deming methods. It explains both theory and application.

**'A useful, easy-to-read guide for employing the master's methods.'** *Los Angeles Times*

# Guides to
# W Edwards Deming's
# Quality Theories (contd)

## Dr Deming – The Man Who Taught the Japanese About Quality
Rafael Aguayo
*(HB, £25.00, 304pp, 234mm x 156mm)*

**'Dr Deming has become synonymous with quality. But the essence of his masterly teaching, excellently expounded in this book, is that quality is synonymous with everything that makes the difference between bad management and very good'**
*Robert Heller*

## The Deming Route To Quality and Productivity
William W Scherkenbach
*(HB, £14.95, 176pp, 234mm x 156mm)*

In 1982, at the recommendation of Dr Deming, William Scherkenbach joined Ford Motor Company with responsibility for guiding the implementation of Deming's philosophies throughout the company. Based on his success at Ford he is now helping General Motors implement the Deming philosophy.

## The Keys To Excellence - The Deming Philosophy
Nancy R Mann
*(HB, £12.95, 156pp, 216mm x 138mm)*

A concise guide, written by the former Vice President of the American Statistical Association.

**'A rattling good read...As clear a message as you're likely to find anywhere'** *Executive Development*

# Global Quality
## The New Management Culture
### John Macdonald & John Piggott

*(HB, £16.95, 224pp, 234mm x 156mm, ISBN~ 5251-039-0)*

*Global Quality* is an established guide to the principles and practices of quality management.

ABOUT THE AUTHORS

John Macdonald is recognised as a pioneer in bringing the quality revolution to Britain. He is a frequent contributor to the national and business press, TV and radio and is a well-known speaker on quality. Having joined forces with Philip Crosby in 1983, he left Crosby Associates in 1988 to write this book and to develop his concepts with consultants Resource Evaluation Ltd.

John Piggott is a member of the Board of Management of the British Quality Association and a member of the Institution of Production Engineers Quality Management Activity Group. In 1989 he helped form the Total Quality Management group of Resource Evaluation Ltd.

'An easy-to-read introduction to TQM...accessible to the typical British manager in a way that some other summaries of this topic are not' *Financial Times*

'An excellent introduction to the theories and practice of TQM' *Virginia Bottomley*

'For those interested in implementing Global Quality this book provides an excellent background' *Total Quality Management*

# But We Are Different!
## Quality For the Service Sector
### John Macdonald

*(HB, £16.95, 224pp, 229mm x 148mm, ISBN: 1-85251-131-1)*

A new guide from the authors of *Global Quality*, applying the pioneering principles of TQM to the service sector.

This book highlights the desperate need for quality improvement in a variety of service organisations. Experience and research shows that the waste of resources in the service sector amounts to more than 30% of operating costs. Additionally the customer is not getting the service he demands. However, a major barrier to progress lies in the service perception that the lessons of quality management only have practical application in manufacturing.

*But We Are Different* (subtitled *Quality Sells Services*) recognises the differences in the service sector and explains them in a wide range of areas. It demonstrates that the principles of TQM are common principles which apply to all organisations. The book describes these principles and then provides a practical guide to their implementation in each area.

ABOUT THE AUTHOR

John Macdonald is recognised as a pioneer in bringing the quality revolution to Britain. He is a frequent contributor to the national and business press, TV and radio and is a well-known speaker on quality. Having joined forces with Philip Crosby in 1983, he left Crosby Associates in 1988 to develop his concepts with consultants Resource Evaluation Limited. He is co-author of *Global Quality*, also available from Management Books 2000.

# The Benchmarking Book
### Michael J Spendolini, PhD

*(HB, £24.95, 224pp, 228mm x 152mm, ISBN: 0-8144-5077-6)*
*(PB, £15.95, 209pp, 228mm x 152mm, ISBN: 0-8144-5077-6)*

*Benchmarking* – the systematic evaluation of the best of the competition – is the new buzzword in quality/product planning.

*The Benchmarking Book* is a definitive synthesis of lessons learned from pioneering benchmarking companies.

Drawing on the experiences of such diverse companies as Boeing, Xerox, AT&T, DuPont, DEC, Motorola and IBM, *The Benchmarking Book* provides anyone interested in the process with the steps they need to establish a benchmarking programme – and a basic model to use or adapt.

The author lays out each major stage of a structured benchmarking process:

- determining which products or processes to benchmark
- forming a benchmarking team
- identifying benchmarking partners
- collecting and analysing benchmarking information
- taking action

*The Benchmarking Book* shows how companies that compare themselves to excellence in others can bring out excellence in themselves.

**'I believe our country needs a new law. No one can utter the word "benchmarking" until they have read carefully Mike Spendolini's The Benchmarking Book'** *Electronics Publishing*

# The Quality Makers
## The Leaders and Shapers of Europe's Quality Revolution
### Robert Heller

*(HB, £25.00, 272pp, 270mm x 195mm, ISBN: 3-907150-47-3)*

Robert Heller charts the development of TQM in Europe with in-depth studies of 20 European organisations that are at the vanguard of the total quality revolution. Companies studied include world-class multi-nationals like Ciba, Rank-Xerox, SGS-Thomson, Groupe Bull, British Telecom, Volkswagen and Societe Generale: divisions or affiliates of leading corporations like Honeywell, British Airways, and American Express; national champions like Italy's Alenia and Britain's Post Office.

ABOUT THE AUTHOR
Robert Heller was the founding editor of *Management Today*, now Britain's leading monthly business magazine. He has written many books, including most recently The Superchiefs (also available from Management Books 2000) and continues to write regularly for a number of leading periodicals.

# The TQM Trilogy

Using ISO 9000, The Deming Prize, and the Baldrige Award to Establish a System for Total Quality Management.

## Francis X Mahoney & Carl Thor

Many managers think that the 'big three' quality standards are only for companies trying to win prizes or pass the test. This book shows how to take advantage of these three models by using them as world-class guidelines for promoting and increasing quality.

Francis Mahoney conducts seminars at the University of Houston. Carl Thor is vice chairman and former president of the American Quality and Productivity Centre and has served as director of the Malcolm Baldrige National Quality Award Consortium.

# Quantum Quality

Quality Improvement Through Innovation, Learning, & Creativity

## William C Miller

*(PB, £17.95, 224pp, 227mm x 152mm, ISBN: 0-8144-7851-4)*

Now that everybody's got the quality message, companies are looking for ways to make progressive quantum leaps in quality improvement. This book shows how to achieve this through the integration of Quality with learning, creativity and innovation.

# The QFD Book

The Team Approach to Solving Problems and Satisfying Customers Through Quality Function Deployment

## Lawrence R Guinta & Nancy C Praizler

*(HB, £24.95, 160pp, 227mm x 153mm, ISBN: 0-8144-5139-X)*

'For a long time I have been looking for a book that explains Quality Function Deployment (QFD) in a logical and easy-to-understand way, and I finally found it' *Quality Digest*